VOLUME 106 OF THE YALE SERIES OF YOUNGER POETS

S L O W

L I G H T N I N G

poems

Eduardo C. Corral

Foreword by Carl Phillips

Yale UNIVERSITY PRESS

New Haven & London

Published with assistance from the Louis Stern Memorial Fund.

Copyright © 2012 by Yale University.

Foreword copyright © 2012 by Carl Phillips.

Yale University Press books may be purchased in quantity for educational, business,
or promotional use. For information, please e-mail sales.press@yale.edu (U.S. office)
or sales@yaleup.co.uk (U.K. office).

Designed by Lindsey Voskowsky.
Set in Bulmer type by Keystone Typesetting, Inc.
Printed in the United States of America.

Library of Congress Cataloging-in-Publication Data
Corral, Eduardo C., 1973–
Slow lightning : poems / Eduardo C. Corral ; foreword by Carl Phillips.
        p.   cm. — (Yale series of younger poets ; volume 106)
    ISBN 978-0-300-17892-0 (hardback)
    ISBN 978-0-300-17893-7 (paperback)
I. Title.
PS3603.O7717S58 2012
811'.6—dc23 2011044948

A catalogue record for this book is available from the British Library.

This paper meets the requirements of ANSI/NISO Z39.48-1992 (Permanence
of Paper).

10 9 8 7 6 5 4

Para mis padres: Higinio & Socorro Corral

CONTENTS

"Before nourishment there must be obedience."

"As my master ate, I ate."

These are the first and last lines, respectively, of Eduardo C. Corral's *Slow Lightning*. We begin and end, then, in some degree of servitude: obedience, enslavement. A frame of sorts. And there's a frame within this one: the second poem in the book is echoed by the penultimate poem, each sharing the title "Acquired Immune Deficiency Syndrome," each poem belying its title, or at best referring to it through surreal (or magically real?) allegory. In the first:

> The deer passes me.
>
> I lower my head,
> stick out my tongue
> to taste

the honey smeared

on its hind leg.

And in the second:

I toss off my robe. A mule

curls its tongue around

my erection. I throw

my head back,

& stare at the slowest lightning,

the stars.

Each scene conflates ritual, nature, the sensuous, the sensual, desire. These become the frame within the outer frame of servitude: servitude-AIDS-AIDS-servitude. Which is to say we have an instance, at the level of imagery and subject matter, of that old Greek rhetorical figure, chiasmus, a frame within a frame, or a cage within a cage—which is why chiasmus tends most often to convey a sense of enclosure, at best; at worst, imprisonment and the claustrophobia that comes with it.

What to make of the various forces and circumstances that cage us in? This is among the underlying questions—perhaps the chief one—throughout *Slow Lightning*. In the first "Acquired Immune Deficiency Syndrome," the speaker finds an abandoned harp and decides to "use the frame as a window/in a chapel/yet to be built," a way of salvaging something useful from apparent ruin. Or consider "The Blindfold," quoted here in its entirety:

I draw the curtains.   The room darkens, but

the mirror still reflects   a crescent moon.

```
I pull        the crescent out,        a rigid curve
that softens                     into a length of cloth
I wrap the cloth around                          my eyes
and I'm peering              through a crack in a wall
revealing                          a landscape of snow.
```

Here, a source of light (doubly reflected) transforms into the tangible, a blindfold that, incongruously, wondrously, becomes the equivalent of a window through which the world can be seen expanding. So we can make of what would blind us a conduit for changed vision, suggests Corral. In these poems, a cage implies all the rest that lies outside it; any frame frames a window through which to see other possibilities unfolding.

One of the more surprising possibilities offered in these poems is joy. Surprising, because the topics visited herein are decidedly sobering ones: the complicated border politics between Mexico and the United States; the ways in which identity both defines us and estranges us—from others as much as from ourselves; the particular agony of unrequited love; the disorientingly thin line between erotic and filial love; that glittering helix, death entwined around desire. But there's a joy that comes across in how the poems are constructed. Code-switching—in this case, the constant shuttling back and forth between Spanish and English—is one of Corral's favorite strategies, most notably in the book's centerpiece, "Variation on a Theme by José Montoya," whose virtuosity and sensibility seem partly an homage, as well, to Langston Hughes's "Montage of a Dream Deferred." Here's an excerpt from the third section of "Variation":

Agringado. Recién llegado.

Eyes the color of garrapatas.

Manos de trapo.

Cell phone strapped like a pistola

to his belt.

His grito: *La revolución no nos hizo iguales.*

The typos he found in menus.

Girled cheese. Trench fries.

Saturday night pachangas.

Western Union

patron.

Drinking piss but dreaming of Patrón.

I see a kind of joy in the playful, acrobatic leaping not just from Spanish to English and back, but from topics like revolution and equality to the humor in the typos on the menu, and from the way more or less the same word can straddle notions of class ("patron") and of having escaped the fetters of class and attained "success" or at least the so-called symbols of it ("Patrón").

And yet, another way of seeing this combination of code-switching and associative leaping is as a form of restlessness, the restlessness perhaps of divided identity, of having nowhere a home especially, or perhaps of finding one's home to be in fact a cage that had gone unnoticed—who put us here? Who are we?

There is also a kind of sorrow, if dreams come down to a brand of liquor, if the pistola's force is now the cell phone's. And if it can be considered an achievement to have become a legal citizen ("Recién llegado"), what to make of the fact that one's fellow citizens can't spell properly in their own language?

Estrangement, Corral suggests, is many-sided. Not to belong anywhere in particular means somehow an ability to go anywhere in general, but always as a tourist, an outsider. The conflation (another form of code-switching), in the sonnet sequence "Border Triptych," of Chicano material and traditional English (i.e., white) prosody is at once an argument for (enactment of) reconciliation and a reminder of the differences, historically, between two cultures. Estrangement is not limited, of course, to race, ethnicity, and language. Corral also examines the ambivalent space between father and son. On one hand:

> You are nothing like my father.
> And like my father
> you are nothing.
> ("To a Jornalero Cleaning Out My Neighbor's Garage")

and on the other:

> I learned to make love to a man
> by touching my father.
>
> . . . .
>
> He would lift me each morning
>
> onto the bathroom counter,
> dot my small palms
>
> with dollops of shaving cream
> so I could lather his face.
>
> ("Ditat Deus")

And there's the estrangement that can equally bind and, over time, destroy two lovers:

                                                    I asked

        once for grace. You dusted

    my face with ash. *I ask, I ask, I ask* . . . You step into the pond.
            Hair dissipating like smoke.

                                        ("To the Beastangel")

and:

            All that glitters isn't music.

            Once, hidden in tall grass,
            I tossed fistfuls of dirt into the air:
            doe after doe of leaping.

            You said it was nothing
            but a trick of the light. Gold
            curves. Gold scarves.

            Am I not your animal?

                                        ("To the Angelbeast")

As Corral notes, the Beastangel and the Angelbeast of the titles of
the two poems above appear in Robert Hayden's "Bone-Flower
Elegy." In many ways, Hayden seems a kind of tutelary god hover-
ing over *Slow Lightning*. Sometimes, it's the Hayden who so poi-
gnantly captured the estrangement of father and son in "Those
Winter Sundays," but more often the Hayden who found himself
caught between identities, decried by the Black Arts Movement as
not being "black" enough, even as he argued for being a poet first,

black second. His masterpiece, "Middle Passage," speaks directly to black history, but not without including references to Shakespeare, Eliot, blank verse tradition—and Negro spirituals. Code-switching, indeed. Like Hayden, Corral resists reductivism. Gay, Chicano, "Illegal-American," that's all just language, and part of Corral's point is that language, like sex, is fluid and dangerous and thrilling, now a cage, now a window out. In Corral's refusal to think in reductive terms lies his great authority. His refusal to entirely trust authority wins my trust as a reader. Intimacy, humor, outrage, longing, fear—and have I mentioned, with no irony whatsoever, the sheer heart of these poems? I love the range here—psychologically, emotionally, but also in terms of mode: narrative, lyric, elegy, homage, the anti-ecphrastic ecphrastic. I love the quiet beauty of language and image, and I love the moments of joyful exuberance, like these from "Self-Portrait with Tumbling and Lasso":

> I'm a cowboy
>
> riding bareback.
> My soul is
> whirling
> above my head like a lasso.
> My right hand
> a pistol. My left
> automatic. I'm knocking
>
> on every door.
> I'm coming on strong . . .

"I'm knocking//on every door./I'm coming on strong . . ." It's hard for me not to think of Plath's poem "Mushrooms," which ends with this declaration: "We shall by morning/Inherit the earth./Our foot's in the door." Corral's voice, his vision—they're every bit as inevitable, it seems to me; as if I'd been waiting all this time to find and be found by them.

Carl Phillips

ACKNOWLEDGMENTS

I would like to thank the editors of the following print and online publications in which these poems, sometimes in different versions, appeared.

Beloit Poetry Journal: "Variation on a Theme by José Montoya"

Black Warrior Review: "Poem after Frida Kahlo's Painting *The Broken Column*"

Devil's Lake: "After Bei Dao/After Jean Valentine"

la fovea: "*La Pelona:* Mixed Media: Ester Hernández: 1980"

Huizache: "Immigration and Naturalization Service Report #46"; "Want"

Indiana Review: "Acquired Immune Deficiency Syndrome [I approach a harp]"

The Journal: "Velvet Mesquite"; "Temple in a Teapot (Aquí Está el Detalle)"

The Laurel Review: "The Blindfold"

The Nation: "Cayucos"

New England Review: "Watermark"

OCHO: "To the Beastangel"

Ploughshares: "Caballero"

Poetry: "To the Angelbeast," "To the Beastangel," "In Colorado My Father Scoured and Stacked Dishes"

Poetry Northwest: "Se Me Olvidó Otra Vez"

Post Road: "All the Trees of the Field Shall Clap Their Hands"; "*Our Completion:* Oil on Wood: Tino Rodríguez: 1999"

Quarterly West: "Acquired Immune Deficiency Syndrome [At a quarter to midnight]"

Salt Hill: "My Hands Are My Heart: Two-Part Cibachrome Print: Gabriel Orozco: 1991"

three candles journal: "Ditat Deus"; "Monologue of a Vulture's Shadow"

Witness: "To a Jornalero Cleaning Out My Neighbor's Garage"; "*Untitled (Perfect Lovers):* Two Commercial Clocks: Felix Gonzalez-Torres: 1987–89"

"All the Trees of the Field Shall Clap Their Hands" was reprinted in *A Face to Meet the Faces: An Anthology of Contemporary Persona Poems,* ed. Stacey Lynn Brown and Oliver de la Paz (Akron: University of Akron Press, 2012).

"Acquired Immune Deficiency Syndrome [I approach a harp]" was reprinted in *A Poet's Craft: The Making and Shaping of Poems,* ed. Annie Finch (Ann Arbor: University of Michigan Press, 2011).

"Monologue of a Vulture's Shadow" was reprinted in *Poems, Poets, Poetry: An Introduction and Anthology*, 3rd edition, ed. Helen Vendler (New York: Bedford/St. Martin's, 2010).

"Se Me Olvidó Otra Vez" was reprinted in *Best New Poets 2006*, ed. Eric Pankey (Charlottesville: Samovar Press, 2006), and in *Beloved on Earth: 150 Poems of Grief and Gratitude*, ed. Jim Perlman, Deborah Cooper, Mara Hart, and Pamela Mittlefehldt (Duluth: Holy Cow Press, 2009).

"Ditat Deus"; "*Misael:* Oil, Acrylic, Mixed Media on Canvas: Julio Galán: 2001"; "Monologue of a Vulture's Shadow"; "Poem after Frieda Kahlo's Painting *The Broken Column*"; and "To a Mojado Who Died Crossing the Desert" were reprinted in *The Wind Shifts: New Latino Poetry*, ed. Francisco Aragón (Tucson: University of Arizona Press, 2007).

"Border Triptych"; "Acquired Immune Deficiency Syndrome [I approach a harp]"; and "Monologue of a Vulture's Shadow" were reprinted in *Digerati: 20 Contemporary Poets in the Virtual World*, ed. Steve Mueske (Burnsville: three candles press, 2006).

"Acquired Immune Deficiency Syndrome [I approach a harp]" was reprinted on *Verse Daily*.

"To a Jornalero Cleaning Out My Neighbor's Garage" was reprinted on *Poetry Daily*.

Web Del Sol published some of these poems online in a chapbook series edited by Bino Realuyo.

For support, encouragement, and advice I wish to thank: Arturo J. Aldama, Naomi Quinonez, Alberto Rios, Norman Dubie, Beckian Fritz Goldberg, Marvin Bell, James Galvin, Mark Levine, Rich Yañez, Rigoberto González, John Olivares Espinoza, Robert Vasquez, Miguel Murphy, Francisco Aragón, Javier O. Huerta, Diana Marie Delgado, Steve Fellner, Manuel Muñoz, C. Dale Young, J. Michael Martinez, David Welch, Tomás Q. Morin, Tom Sleigh, Peter Balakian, Jennifer Brice, Shara McCallum, and Raquel Vigueria.

Carl Phillips: Salamat. Danke. Gracias. Merci.

For generous gifts of shelter and sustenance I'm indebted to: Canto-Mundo, the Bread Loaf Writers' Conference, the Hall Farm Center, the MacDowell Colony, the Virginia Center for the Creative Arts, and Yaddo.

This book would not exist without the time and space afforded by the Olive B. O'Connor Fellowship in Creative Writing at Colgate University and the Philip Roth Residence in Creative Writing at Bucknell University.

OUR COMPLETION: OIL ON WOOD: TINO RODRÍGUEZ: 1999

Before nourishment there must be obedience.
In his hands I was a cup overflowing with thirst.
Eighth ruler of my days, ninth lord of my nights:
he thrashed above me, like branches. Once,
after weeks of rain, he sliced a potato in half
to remind me of the moon. The dark slept in the small
of his back. The back of his knees: pale music.
We'd crumble the Eucharist & feed it to the pigeons.
Sin vergüenza. Escuintle. He Who Makes Things Sprout.
In the margins in a book of poems by Emily Dickinson
he scribbled: *she had a pocketful of horses/Trojan/
& some of them used.* Often I mistook him for a storyteller
when he stood in the rain. A su izquierda, huesos.
A su derecha, mapas de cuero. When I'd yawn,
he'd pluck black petals out of my mouth.

ACQUIRED IMMUNE DEFICIENCY SYNDROME

I approach a harp
    abandoned
in a harvested field.
    A deer leaps
out of the brush
    and follows me

in the rain, a scarlet
    snake wound
in its dark antlers.
    My fingers
curled around a shard
    of glass—

it's like holding the hand
    of a child.
I'll cut the harp strings
    for my mandolin,
use the frame as a window
    in a chapel
yet to be built. I'll scrape

    off its blue
lacquer, melt the flakes

down with
a candle and ladle
and paint
the inner curve
of my soup bowl.

The deer passes me.
I lower my head,
stick out my tongue
to taste
the honey smeared
on its hind leg.

In the field's center
I crouch near
a boulder engraved
with a number
and stare at a gazelle's
blue ghost,
the rain falling through it.

In the dark only the Devil can cast a shadow.

Too poor to afford lilies,
she walked down the aisle holding a glass of milk.

Her left breast
is nicknamed Juan. The right, Diego.

Nightly she catches moths
with newspaper cones.

Hammock Skipper. Southern Emerald.
Lungs black with cancer, her father

was buried two months
before the wedding.

Co coo coo roo. Her name a tassel
in my mouth: *Socorro, Socorro.*

Rain pierced her womb
when she was six months pregnant. Rain

singed
the face of her child.

The burn marks turning
into beauty marks. Beautiful flaw.

Terrible ornament.
I keep a spur under my pillow to ward off nightmares.

Too poor
to afford lace,

she walked down the aisle

on a cold afternoon, her breath a veil.

                                  She arranges moth wings on a table,
reads the wings

                                                      like Tarot cards.
Nine of Swords. Knight of Coins.

                            Her mouth waters when she hears
a bolero. *Co coo coo roo.*

                                        Her father was buried
in pleated pants.

                                              Day after day
she folds and folds paper. Alas. Faros.

                            She gave me a pack of cigarettes
on my thirteenth birthday.

                                                        Often
I put on the gold ring she leaves by the sink.

                                        Not cathedrals
but presence.

                            The first man she saw naked
was the rain. The dark of her knees

                                              a watermark.
Socorro, Socorro.

                            If I dream I'm cupping her face
with my hands, I wake up holding

                                              the skull
of a wolf.

THE BLINDFOLD

I draw the curtains.   The room darkens, but
the mirror still reflects   a crescent moon.
I pull   the crescent out,   a rigid curve
that softens   into a length of cloth.
I wrap the cloth around   my eyes,
and I'm peering   through a crack in a wall
revealing   a landscape of snow.

IN COLORADO MY FATHER SCOURED AND STACKED DISHES

in a Tex-Mex restaurant. His co-workers,
unable to utter his name, renamed him Jalapeño.

If I ask for a goldfish, he spits a glob of phlegm
into a jar of water. The silver letters

on his black belt spell *Sangrón*. Once, borracho,
at dinner, he said: Jesus wasn't a snowman.

Arriba Durango. Arriba Orizaba. Packed
into a car trunk, he was smuggled into the States.

Frijolero. Greaser. In Tucson he branded
cattle. He slept in a stable. The horse blankets

oddly fragrant: wood smoke, lilac. He's an illegal.
I'm an Illegal-American. Once, in a grove

of saguaro, at dusk, I slept next to him. I woke
with his thumb in my mouth. ¿No qué no

tronabas pistolita? He learned English
by listening to the radio. The first four words

he memorized: In God We Trust. The fifth:
Percolate. Again and again I borrow his clothes.

He calls me Scarecrow. In Oregon he picked apples.
Braeburn. Jonagold. Cameo. Nightly,

to entertain his cuates, around a campfire,
he strummed a guitarra, sang corridos. Arriba

Durango. Arriba Orizaba. Packed into
a car trunk, he was smuggled into the States.

Greaser. Beaner. Once, borracho, at breakfast,
he said: The heart can only be broken

once, like a window. ¡No mames! His favorite
belt buckle: an águila perched on a nopal.

If he laughs out loud, his hands tremble.
Bugs Bunny wants to deport him. César Chávez

wants to deport him. When I walk through
the desert, I wear his shirt. The gaze of the moon

stitches the buttons of his shirt to my skin.
The snake hisses. The snake is torn.

MISAEL: OIL, ACRYLIC, MIXED MEDIA ON CANVAS: JULIO GALÁN: 2001

again and again he shuffled a deck of cards/a small accordion

in his hands/to be a man/ to be a tree/or even something less/like a plank

the wounds along his shoulder/salmon leaping out of black water

BORDER TRIPTYCH

1

For the past fifteen years, six days a week, at half past eight,
Jorge has biked into my checkpoint station. He hawks
over his papers, allows me to examine his lunch box,
& then wheels off to his twelve hour shift at the pallet & crate

factory. I'm close to madness. I suspect
he's been smuggling contraband, prescription or illegal.
He sports new toupees under a cap depicting an eagle
devouring a snake. He rides spit-shined bikes that I inspect

by taking them apart, checking inside the hollow
pipes, sometimes slicing open the tires, but so far nothing.
Jorge always remains calm, & doesn't say a damn thing.
Yesterday, a few days from my retirement, I swallowed

my pride, & swore, if he told me the truth, to keep my lips tight.
The bastard smiled, & casually replied, I smuggle bikes.

2

INS transcript, Sofia: I kept my mother's advice
to myself. Before crossing the Tijuana/San Diego border,
in a bathroom stall, I sprinkled gelatin powder
on my underwear. We slipped through a fence like mice,

& waited in a neighborhood park. Hourly, vans
arrived, & we were packed in, driven up river-wide asphalt
toward families, jobs. Sweat soaked our clothes, salted
our skin. We stopped on an isolated road. Bandits

stepped from the trees. The men were forced face down
in a ravine. The women were ordered to undress at gunpoint.
I unbuckled my belt, lowered my jeans. Sweat,
gelatin powder had stained my underwear a reddish brown.

I was one of ten women. Our mouths were taped.
I was spit on. I was slapped. The other women were raped.

3

Sapo & I wait for the cool of night under mesquite.

Three days in the desert & we're still too close to Mexico,

still so far from God. Sapo's lips so dry he swabs the pus leaking

from the ampollas on his toes across his mouth. I flip a peso.

Heads: we continue. Tails: we walk toward the highway,

thumb our way back to Nogales. The peso disappears into a nest

but the hard-on in Sapo's jeans, slightly curved, points west.

I catch a cascabel & strip off its meat. Sapo mutters, No que no guey.

I bury its forked tongue: for one night our names won't flower

in the devil's throat. We're Indios but no grin-

go will mistake us for Navajos. Above us, an owl grins

like Cantinflas. The arms of the saguaros strike down the hours

but the sun refuses to set. Sapo shits behind a cluster of nopales,

& shouts out our favorite joke, No tengo papeles!

for Gloria Anzaldúa

14

LA PELONA: MIXED MEDIA:
ESTER HERNÁNDEZ: 1980

fist of ice skin trellis pagan rubble whistling ash

a phrase turning up the dark salt's rattle arctic

ruca centuries cut and crushed cocaine terrace

thumbed gold flock of knots chafoso grammar

woven moth-dust an egg cracking into arabic

as pretty as a gust Xquic's blood collar a fable

braided and quickly dressed in milk boneflower

IMMIGRATION AND NATURALIZATION SERVICE REPORT #46

After the body was bagged and whisked away, we noticed a scarlet pelt on the sand. "This guy had it nice, sleeping on a pelt for days," Ignacio joked. He paused mid-laugh, bent down, ran his hand through the fur. One of his fingers snagged. "This isn't a pelt, it's a patch of wolf ears," he said. "No, they're too large," I replied. "Then they must be coyote ears," he murmured. Sweat gathered in the small of my back. "Ignacio, should we radio headquarters?" I asked. Two ears rose slowly from the patch. I said a few more words. Nothing. I uttered my own name. Two more ears unfurled. We stepped back from the patch, called out the names of our fathers and mothers. Ramón. Juana. Octavio. More and more ears rose. Rodolfo. Gloria . . .

for Javier O. Huerta

WANT

abandoned by his coyote, my
father, sand seething beneath
his sneakers,   trekked
through   southern Arizona:
maze of acacia   & cholla
cold sweat cut   his face like
a razor   in his pocket: a fine-
tooth comb, dice, & a photo
of a girl playing a violin   on
the third day,   he picked up
a rock,   killed a blue lizard
with a single strike he tore it
apart,   shoved guts & bones
into his mouth   the first
time I knelt for a man,   my
lips   pressed to his zipper,
I suffered   such hunger

AFTER BEI DAO/AFTER JEAN VALENTINE

The skin of your deity smells like gasoline

Your prayers are added to the pyre

A gold wheel spinning

Once your voice broke out in a sweat

Each word a salt lick

There are fingers rooting inside a violin

Orchestral maneuvers

In the middle of the pandemic

You mistook a group of ghosts for an orchard

You, coward

Fingers are rooting inside a violin to pull out

The last scraps of birdsong

A gold wheel spinning in your mind

Like insomnia

SE ME OLVIDÓ OTRA VEZ

I sit in bed, from the linen your scent still rises.
You're asleep inside your old guitar.

A mariachi suit draped on a chair, its copper buttons,
the eyes of jaguars stalking the night.

I sit in bed, from the linen your scent still rises.

Through a window a full moon brings to mind Borges,
there is such loneliness in that gold.

You're asleep inside your old guitar.

Are your calloused heels scraping its curved wood or
are there mice scurrying in the walls?

I sit in bed, from the linen your scent still rises.

I flick on a lamp, yellow light strikes your guitar
like dirt thrown on a coffin.

You're asleep inside your old guitar.
I sit in bed, from the linen your scent still rises.

after Donald Justice

SELF-PORTRAIT WITH TUMBLING AND LASSO

I'm drumroll and voyeur.
    I'm watermark
and fable. I'm weaving
    the snarls
of a wolf through my hair
    like ribbon. At my feet,
chisels

    and jigsaws. I'm
performing
    an autopsy on my shadow.
My rib cage a wall.
    My heart
a crack in a wall,
    a foothold. I'm tumbling

upward:
    a French acrobat. I'm judder
and effigy.
    I'm pompadour
and splendid. I'm spinning
    on a spit, split
in half.

An apple
in my mouth. I know
    what Eve
didn't know: a serpent
    is a fruit eaten to the core. I'm
a massacre
    of the dreamers,

a terra cotta soldier
    waiting for
his emperor's return.
    When I bow,
a black fish leaps
    from the small of my back.
I catch it.

    I tear it apart. I fix
the scales
    to my lips.
Every word I utter
    is opalescent. I'm skinned
and Orphic.
    I'm scarlet

and threshold. At my touch,
    a piano
melts like a slab
    of black ice. I'm
steam rising,
    dissipating. I'm a ghost undressing.
I'm a cowboy

riding bareback.
My soul is
    whirling
above my head like a lasso.
    My right hand
a pistol. My left
    automatic. I'm knocking

on every door.
    I'm coming on strong,
like a missionary.
    I'm kicking back
my legs, like a mule. I'm kicking up
    my legs, like
a showgirl.

POEM AFTER FRIDA KAHLO'S PAINTING *THE BROKEN COLUMN*

1

On a bench, beneath a candle-lit window
whose sheer curtains resemble honey
sliding down a jar, Kahlo lifts her skirts.

A brown monkey chews a tobacco leaf
between her legs, tail brushing her thigh.
A skirt falls; the hem splashes on the floor

like urine. A ruby ring on her forefinger.
No, the tip of a cigarette. Smoke rising.
The long hair of an old woman drowning.

2

Once a man offered me his heart like a glass of water. No, once . . . Here's a joke for you. Why do Mexicans make tamales at Christmas? So they have something to unwrap. A lover told me that. I stared into his eyes believing the brown surrounding his pupils were rings, like Saturn's. I have to sit down to say this. Once a man offered me his heart and I said no. Not because I didn't love him. Not because he was a beast or white—I couldn't love him. Do you understand? In bed while we slept, our bodies inches apart, the dark between our flesh a wick. It was burning down. And he couldn't feel it.

3

Ask me anything.

4

I want to find the perfect shade of red. Say that.

5

A shadow drapes itself on an apple branch. Slow. Slowly. Jade moss on the trunk intensifies like applause. Wind-braid wrapped around my neck, unraveling: cold hair cascading toward my shoulders.

6

Ladies and Gentlemen once again I would like to begin with the wound.

—Joseph Beuys

7

Diego sleeps!

Green sheets pulled down to his waist.

A fly lands on his left eyelid,

and for a moment

it looks like one eye is open.

A monkey jumps

onto the bed, begins to lick the sweat

in the hollow of his chest.

8

Constellations of coins scatter copper and silver light onto the butcher paper taped above a dresser. Crystal pitcher full of milk, arranged with lilies.

Torn sketch on the floor.

Through the window, sky like a torn sketch of the ocean.

Kahlo glaring at a self-portrait
as if her gaze were responsible for holding it to the wall.

9

The perfect shade of red:
the stain on an arrow pulled out of a dove.

10

Under the cold scaffolding of winter my love took me for a walk through the desert. My breath crumbling like bread.

Under the cold scaffolding of winter my love took me for a stroll through the desert. My breath crumbling like bread.

Under the cold scaffolding of winter my love took me through the desert. My breath crumbling like bread.

11

Kahlo undresses in front of a mirror.

Her spine: a pouring of sand

through an hourglass

of blood.

Her hands

clutching the linen

draping the lower half

of her body, her fingers lost in its pleats.

12

A mirror remembering water.

CAYUCOS

boats used by African emigrants
to reach Spanish islands

A girl asleep beneath a fishing net

Sandals the color of tangerines

Off the coast of Morocco

A moonlit downpour, God's skeleton

Bark, dory, punt, skiff

"Each with a soul full of scents"

Day after day spent shaping

A ball of wax into a canary

Little lamp, little lamp

The word "contraband" arrived

In English in the 16th century via Spanish

Throw your shadow overboard

Proverbs, blessings scratched into wood

The tar of my country better than the honey of others

VARIATION ON A THEME BY JOSÉ MONTOYA

Hoy enterraron al Monchie.
El Mero Mero de Durango. Mister
No Contaron con Mi Astucia.

They found his body
    afuera de Eloy,
debajo de un mesquite.

Hands tied,
    a bullet to the cabeza.
Dicen que murió

por el polvo.
    Tell los chismosos
he pushed a lawnmower

in Palo Alto.
    Tell los chismosos
he flipped burgers

in Sacramento.
    Tell los chismosos naco
but not narco.

and blackness ahead and when shall I reach

(the trumpet cries)

that somewhere

morning and keep on going

(the accordion moans)

and never turn back

and keep on going

(the trumpet wails)

Agringado. Recién llegado.

Eyes the color of garrapatas.

Manos de trapo.

Cell phone strapped like a pistola

to his belt.

His grito: *La revolución no nos hizo iguales.*

The typos he found in menus.

Girled cheese. Trench fries.

Saturday night pachangas.

Western Union

patron.

Drinking piss but dreaming of Patrón.

"Al pie de un verde nopal yo me acosté/
Al ruido de unas guitarras yo me dormí."

Camisa negra. Gold necklaces.

Dólar

store cologne.

La pinche migra at every pinche corner.

The batteries

for his radio. Los Yonics. Los Bukis.

A small apartment. Six roommates.

"Adiós paisanos queridos/ Ya nos van a deportar."

Prepaid

phonecards. Flea market bicycles.

Above his heart, an alacrán tattoo.

Pocho words

like pepper on his lengua. Hina. Pichear.

With a marker he'd scrawl *Viva Colosio*

on his apron.

Agringado. Recién llegado.

35

overturned rocks   *hoy*

                        water splashes on canal walls

the whirl of helicopter blades   *me*

                voy   indigo-peaked mountains

scorpionweed/puncture vine   *hoy*

                        old wagon trails/hiking paths

ruthless north star

                                water stations

sardine tins/plastic bags   *hoy*

                        infrared sensors/sound detectors

morning several hours away by foot   *me*

                        voy

Near Douglas,

on a gabacho's rancho,

he found

a scarecrow

decked out

in the uniform

of a border agent.

Using blood

and papel

he made a note

that he hung

around its neck

that read: *Pancho*

Was Here.

Qué chido his chistes. Qué
chido his tocayo. Qué
chido his peso-colored balas. Qué
chido his mandas. Qué
chido his snakeskin botas. Qué
chido his guitarra. Qué
chido his rolas. Qué
chido his Chalino t-shirts. Qué
chido his botellas. Qué
chido his lust for tetas. Qué
chido his puros. Qué
chido his carcajadas. Qué
chido his golfas. Qué
chido his reloj de plata. Qué
chido his groserías. Qué
chido his copitas de mezcal. Qué
chido his billetes. Qué
chido his puñetadas. Qué
chido his bigote. Qué
chido his cuerno de chivo. Qué
chido his piropos. Qué
chido his tarjetas telefónicas. Qué
chido his pachangas. Qué
chido his antojos. Qué
chido his pasitos Duranguense. Qué
chido his gallos. Qué
chido his rompecabezas. Qué
chido his grito.

Marooned in salmon-

morning

colored sand, surrounded

and keep on going

by desert marigolds

and never turn back

and sotol, a rusty '68 Impala:

and blackness a wetback's motel.

ahead

The sun rising

in the rearview mirror. Bucket

morning

scats torn out. In the trunk, on a pile

and keep on going   of tattered jackets,

and never turn back

an acoustic guitar

and blackness

like a mischievous girl lifting

ahead

her dress.

Hoy enterraron al Monchie.
El Mero Mero de Durango. Mister
No Contaron con Mi Astucia.

His brothers
    carried his black caja
through las calles
    of Orizaba.

They dressed him
    in a Dodgers jersey,
necklaces de oro,
    snakeskin botas.

Before digging
    under a mulberry,
his cuates poured
    caguamas

on the ground
    to loosen the earth.
His caja was lowered slowly
    into the dark.

Instead of dirt
    his jefe tossed
a fistful of silver bullets
    on the caja.

porque no quiero olvidar me voy me voy

(the trumpet cries)

a Los Angeles porque no quiero olvidar

me voy a Los Angeles me voy

(the accordion moans)

a Los Angeles porque no quiero olvidar

mi México

(the trumpet wails)

ع

CABALLERO

Only symmetry harbors loss.
   —Lorna Dee Cervantes

 Throatlatch.
Crupper. Martingale. Terret. My breath
  tightens around him,
    like a harness. Once a year
he eats a spoonful of dirt
 from his father's grave.

    In his sleep
   he mutters lines
    from his favorite flick,
   Capulina

Contra Los Vampiros.
Summers he hunts underground water with a
  dowsing rod made
    from the sun-bleached spine
of a wolf. When a word stalls
 on his tongue he utters,

    Sufferin succotash.
   Stout. Apache-
    dark. Curious
  and quick.

He builds up the bridge
of his nose with clay. Mornings he sings: Dices
                 que me quieres pero
                                mi tienes trabajando. He spits
        into a tin cup each time
            lightning strikes. In the small
                                of his back I bury
                            my hands. Once,
                                lost in the desert,
                            he ate beak-

        punctured pitayas;
pissed on his fingers to keep them warm. Weekly
                he plays poker with other
                                mojados. The winning hands
        teach him more English. Sawmill.
            Three Kings. Presto.

                            He pronounces
                        my name beautifully.
                                His thumb: flecha
                    de sal,

        gancho de menta.
In Nogales he bought a whisky-colored mutt.
                He named it Nalgas.
                            He slipped a canary into
        his father's coffin: its pecking,
            its hunger, smoothing
                                the creases

of the face.

With an old sock
and black coffee

he polishes his boots.
Rosa salvaje. Corazón salvaje. The inner-
most part of a castle
is the keep. Andale, pues.
When I ride him at night I call out
the name of his first horse.

DITAT DEUS

1

In high school I worked as a bag boy. To prevent shoplifting my boss had me follow the Mexicans & the Native Americans who came in to shop. I was slightly troubled by this. So I only followed the handsome men.

2

I learned to make love to a man
by touching my father.

I would unlace his work boots,
pull off his socks,

& drag my thumbs
along the arches of his feet.

When he slept I would trace
the veins of his neck,

blue beneath my fingertip.
He would lift me each morning

onto the bathroom counter,
dot my small palms

with dollops of shaving cream
so I could lather his face.

ALL THE TREES OF THE FIELD
SHALL CLAP THEIR HANDS

Josefa Segovia was tried, convicted & hanged on July 5, 1851, in Downieville, California, for killing an Anglo miner, a man who the day before had assaulted her.

Are the knees & elbows
    the first knots
        the dead untie?
  I swing from a rope
    lashed
to a beam. Some men
along the Yuba river
    toss coins
    into the doubling water.
    Visible skin.
    Memorable hair.
Imagine: coal, plow,
    rust, century.
  All layers
of the same palabra.
        Once
I mistook a peach pit
    on a white dish
    for a thumbprint.
Wolf counselor.

Reaper.

Small rock.

The knot just under

my right ear

whispers *God is gracious,*

God will

increase. The soul,

like semen,

escapes

the body

swiftly.

TO THE BEASTANGEL

> . . . *unconscionable musics*
> —Ronald Johnson

A pouring of milk among the reeds, the neck of a swan. I float
   on a pond. Nude. Obese. Around

my throat, on a leather cord, an amulet carved from soap.
   Myth-haired, eyes shut,

you stand on the bank. In your hands a finch. I call your name.
   You release the finch. It wings toward me,

settles on my chest. It pecks and pecks at the moles on my skin,
   swallows the moles

like seeds. I asked once for a father. You gave me a wreath.
   I asked once for a sonnet. You

peeled back the skin and muscle of your left hand: fourteen bones.
   One by one the moles

on my body disappear. Leaving me immaculate. Leaving me
   ravenous. I call your name. The finch

flies back to you. You crush it. Bright blood, blue guts. I asked
   once for grace. You dusted

my face with ash. *I ask, I ask, I ask* . . . You step into the pond.
   Hair dissipating like smoke.

Eyes still shut. The reeds tick and tick. At your touch, my nipples
   open like bird beaks.

TO THE ANGELBEAST

All that glitters isn't music.

Once, hidden in tall grass,
I tossed fistfuls of dirt into the air:
doe after doe of leaping.

You said it was nothing
but a trick of the light. Gold
curves. Gold scarves.

Am I not your animal?

You'd wait in the orchard for hours
to watch a deer
break from the shadows.

You said it was like lifting a cello
out of its black case.

for Arthur Russell

MY HANDS ARE MY HEART: TWO-PART
CIBACHROME PRINT: GABRIEL OROZCO:
1991

1. Often I catch him playing doctor with his shadow.

2. Por arriba, por abajo.

3. With duct tape he mends his favorite jeans.

4. The way stubble salts his chin.

5. A saxophone is nothing like an ampersand in his hands.

6. Hound & brassbound.

7. Above his mattress there's a poster of a Ferris wheel.

8. Ripped jeans. Paint-streaked boots.

9. Las tardes aquellas.

10. In his wallet a fake driver's license.

11. Plumed initials.

12. To make an animal out of tenderness.

13. Aztec. Trekkie. AZT.

14. To run through the corridors of a corrido.

15. Like bitter water, like burning water.

16. ¡Que jale!

17. The way the light touches him, like a priest.

18. Thumb to chin, thumb to forehead.

19. Du wah. Du wah.

20. He believes a pomegranate is a thesaurus.

21. Each seed a synonym for the color red.

22. Garnet. Puce. Claret.

23. To dig a little in this world.

24. Like the song-limbed.

25. His mouth is nothing like a cup.

26. Impossible to drink from, impossible to shatter.

27. Pero que necesidad.

28. After a meal he plucks a cigarillo from his pocket.

29. Though rain collects in the small of his back.

30. Even music can bleed.

31. To crash a quinceañera just for the quesadillas.

32. Codo. Baboso. Pendejo.

33. Sometimes I gather the vowels in his last name.

34. Acquired. *Acquired.*

35. He carries the scent of musk around like a musket.

36. My minuteman.

TEMPLE IN A TEAPOT
(AQUÍ ESTÁ EL DETALLE)

She grew marijuana
in the garden.

If chickens
ate her crop,

she strangled them,
made a stew.

ξ

to cure her insomnia
she crushed a few verbs
into dust,
scattered the dust
around the bed

to soothe her broken heart
she burned the photos and letters,
kept an adjective
as a memento

ξ

Her specialty? Satin, lace, sequins. Plunging necklines. Once, eight years old, I stood on a crate near the stove. She walked around and around me—a joint in her mouth. Each time she exhaled she placed her lips close to my skin. The smoke clung to my body. She slowly worked the sketch out in her mind. Slowly, she dressed me in a gown of smoke.

ξ

After her left foot was cut off,

still a little groggy,

she asked a nurse if she could take it home,

wrapped in foil.

ξ

those who refused to eat fruit
were scolded *a map*
a day keeps the doctor away

each time she'd break up
a skirmish she'd yell
this is nothing but a temple
in a teapot

ξ

In a photograph she's a mound of salt.
In a photograph she's a slaughterhouse, a rack of meat.
In a photograph she's an umbilical cord.
In a photograph she's a little mirror moving through a forest.
In a photograph she's a scattering of jade.

ξ

I said: Oh
the things that
come out
of your mouth.

She said: Oh
the things
that go into your
mouth.

ξ

canaries flit from branch to branch in a pear tree

wing bones knitting the blood inside their bodies

into the ruby handkerchiefs in the breast pockets

of the handsome men who shouldered her coffin

ξ

TO A JORNALERO CLEANING OUT
MY NEIGHBOR'S GARAGE

You are nothing like my father.

                       And like my father

you are nothing.

                    Zambo. Castizo.

Without draft animals

        the Mexica used the wheel

                        only as a toy.

Please keep off the lawn.

              Green mirrors are asleep

beneath the grass.

          In graduate school a landlord asked,

Here to pick strawberries?

             "Y me vine de Hermosillo/

en busca de oro y riqueza."

                    Are your hands

always so dirty?

            Slip a finger in my mouth.

I'll devour the grime

        under the nail.

             Pomegranate, grenade.

Sometimes in order to say a word

                it's necessary

to spit it out. *A spic sells seashells*

          on the seashore. Corrido singers

often consider assonance

                                 a blemish.

You walk out with a French horn in your arms

                                        and you're a butcher

in El Dorado holding

               the golden entrails of cattle.

for John Olivares Espinoza

TO ROBERT HAYDEN

Less lonely, less . . .

I gave you
a tiny box.
You lifted the lid,
praised
the usefulness
of my gift:
a silver pin shaped
like an amper-
sand. As you fastened it
to your lapel,
I thought again of
that motel
outside of Chicago.
¿Te acuerdas?
I sat on the edge
of a bench,
untied my shoes.
Face down, eyes shut,
you breathed in
the aroma
of sweat & allspice
coming off

the sheets. I tossed
my ring—gold,
inscribed—toward a pile
of clothes.
But the ring
dropped in the small
of your back
where it rattled
& rattled like a coin
in a beggar's
cup.

VELVET MESQUITE

early   in the morning
he gathers   gloves
and   burlap sacks
I pour   whiskey
into his flask   I
search for the pickup's
keys   the engine
stalls as he   turns
the ignition   I shout
a few   words *arroyo*
socorro   *arroz*
the rolled r's   coax
the engine into a roar

ξ

once I chased a stench
through a grove   of
saguaro in a   patch
of grass   I found
the carcass of an ash-
colored coyote   a
gash   jagging its pelt
I knelt   touched its

ears and snout   my
face   rippled beneath
my fingers   as if I
were troubling   water

ξ

winter deciduous bark
stripped braided   in-
to rope   yellow
green leaves   forking
trunk   nurse tree

ξ

he stacks   branches
I   haul sacks of mes-
quite pods   shirtless
worn-out we rest   in
the shade   I draw
squares in the   sand
with   bottle caps
we play checkers   if
our   fingers touch
*en passant   king's
gambit*   the scorpion
on his belt   buckle
raises its silver   tail

for my father

TO A MOJADO WHO DIED
CROSSING THE DESERT

After a storm saguaros glisten
                like mint trombones.
     Sometimes a coyote leaps
over creosote.
        Hush.
The sand calls out for more footprints.
          A crack in a boulder
can never be an entrance
               to a cathedral
but a mouse can be torn open
          like an orange.
Hush.
     The arroyo is the color of rust.
          Sometimes a gust of snow
floats across the water
       as gracefully as a bride.

SAINT ANTHONY'S CHURCH

Instead of a large oak door, a loom. Instead of mosaic windows, wedges of fruit. Instead of a poor box, a loaf of bread. Instead of holy water, gin.

Instead of pews, beds. Instead of hymns, gossip. Instead of the Stations of the Cross, instructions on how to build a kite out of canvas, sticks.

Instead of an altar, a butcher's table. Instead of the nailed palms of Christ, my father's warm hand on my shoulder.

UNTITLED (PERFECT LOVERS): TWO COMMERCIAL CLOCKS: FELIX GONZALEZ-TORRES: 1987-89

a sentence bleeding milk

to burn like the lost

darner amberwing skimmer

the light of the next door

after hunger a watermark

in armor in lilac

music in the mirrors

sleeping but falling

nightly the fragrant hymns

prophecies like salt

torn ram tar mint star thorn

rain in the throat

to leap over the hours

vague gods small truths

to scatter the golden dirt

ACQUIRED IMMUNE DEFICIENCY SYNDROME

At a quarter to midnight,
blue beetles crawling
along the minute hand
of the wall clock,
I awaken, panicked,
next to my lover,

a caramel-hued cello asleep
on embroidered linen.
A light bulb blazes,
burns out,
a doe's flash of white tail
that instructs

the fawn to follow its mother
in flight. I hurry down
a hallway, through a door,
into a pasture
where mules are grazing.
Moonlight

floats in the air like coarse cloth,
silver-speckled
& woven on the looms

of mirrors. Once
      I tore into the torso of my cello
        & discovered

      its heart: a pair of horse shoes
caked with red clay.
        The mules surround me:
necks bent,
      nostrils pluming out different lengths
        of breath.

      I toss off my robe. A mule
curls its tongue around
        my erection. I throw
my head back,
      & stare at the slowest lightning,
        the stars.

MONOLOGUE OF A VULTURE'S SHADOW

I long to return to my master
    who knew neither fear nor patience.
My master who years ago spiraled
    above a woman
trudging through the desert.
    She raised her face & cursed us:
        Black Torches of Plague, Turd Blossoms.
She lashed out with her hands,
    pinned me to her shoulders.
        I went slack.
I called for my master.
    I fell across her shoulders like a black shawl.
Now I'm kept on the shelf of an armoire:
    perfumed,
        my edges embroidered with red thread.
She anchors me to her dress with a cameo of a bird
    clutching prey
as if to remind me of when my master flew close to the desert floor
    & I darkened the arroyos
        & the jade geometry of fallen saguaros.
How could I forget?
    Sometimes my master soared so high
    I ceased to blacken the earth.

What became of me in those moments?

        But the scent of decay always lured my master

            earthward.

As my master ate, I ate.

NOTES

"*Our Completion: Oil on Wood: Tino Rodríguez: 1999*" borrows lyrics from "Little Red Corvette," a song written by Prince.

"Watermark" borrows two phrases from Gwendolyn Brooks's "A Boy Breaking Glass."

"Misael: Oil, Acrylic, Mixed Media on Canvas: Julio Galan: 2001" borrows and alters language from Humberto Ak'abal's "At the Side of the Road."

"Se Me Olvidó Otra Vez" borrows language from Jorge Luis Borges's "The Moon."

"Cayucos" borrows language from Maria Meléndez's "Remedio."

"Variation on a Theme by José Montoya" borrows language from Robert Hayden's "Runagate, Runagate" and from a border folk song and a corrido, "El Crudo" and "El Deportado."

The Angelbeast and the Beastangel are invoked at the end of Robert Hayden's "Bone-Flower Elegy."

"All the Trees of the Field Shall Clap Their Hands" borrows two phrases from Toni Morrison's *Beloved*. Some of the details are taken from online articles about the incident.

"To a Jornalero Cleaning Out My Neighbor's Garage" borrows language from a Joaquin Murrieta corrido, Angela de Hoyos's "Semantics," and Américo Paredes's *With His Pistol in His Hand*.

The epigraph to "To Robert Hayden" comes from Robert Hayden's "The Mirages."

"*Untitled (Perfect Lovers):* Two Commercial Clocks: Felix Gonzalez-Torres: 1987–89" borrows and alters language from Luis Omar Salinas's "Late Evening Conversation with My Friend's Dog Moses, After Watching Visconti's *The Innocent*."